QED

A PLAY

by Peter Parnell

Inspired by the writings of
Richard Feynman, and Ralph Leighton's
Tuva Or Bust!

With a foreword by
Alan Alda

APPLAUSE
THEATRE & CINEMA BOOKS

QED: A Play
by Peter Parnell

Library of Congress Cataloguing-in-Publication Data:

Parnell, Peter.
QED : a play / by Peter Parnell ; inspired by the writings of Richard Feynman, and Ralph Leighton's Tuva or bust!.
p. cm.
ISBN 1-55783-592-6
1. Feynman, Richard Phillips--Drama. 2. Quantum electro-dynamics--Drama. 3. Cancer--Patients--Drama. 4. Terminally ill--Drama. 5. Atomic bomb--Drama. 6. Physicists--Drama. I. Feynman, Richard Phillips. II. Leighton, Ralph. Tuva or bust!.
III. Title.
PS3566.A752Q43 2002
812'.54--dc21

2002008311

British Library Cataloguing-in-Publication Data:
A catalogue record for this book is available from the British Library

Applause Theatre & Cinema Books
151 West 46th Street, 8th Floor
New York, NY 10036
Phone: (212) 575-9265
Fax: (646) 562-5852
email: info@applausepub.com
internet: www.applausepub.com

SALES & DISTRIBUTION

North America:
HAL LEONARD CORP.
7777 West Bluemound Road
P.O. Box 13819
Milwaukee, WI 53213
Phone: (414) 774-3630
Fax: (414) 774-3259

UK:
COMBINED BOOK SERVICES LTD.
Units I/K, Paddock Wood Distribution Centre
Paddock Wood, Tonbridge, Kent TN12 6UU
United Kingdom
Phone: (44) 01892 837171
Fax: (44) 01892 837272

email: halinfo@halleonard.com
internet: www.halleonard.com

Finding Feynman
by Alan Alda

(adapted from his talk at the Caltech commencement, June, 2002)

Twenty-five or thirty years ago, on my days off from the Korean War, which was at that time being waged at Twentieth Century Fox in Beverly Hills, I would often drive to Pasadena to visit the Rembrandts at the Norton Simon Gallery, or take a walk in the Huntington Gardens. And sometimes I would drive by Caltech and give it a glance and wonder what interesting stuff was going on in there. I had been reading avidly about science for years and I was immensely curious about how scientists went about what they did. It didn't occur to me each time I passed by that there was one particular man in one of those buildings who at that moment might have been drawing gluon tubes on a blackboard, or playing the bongos, or just standing looking out the window as a young woman passed by—a man in whom, in a few years, I would become intensely interested.

I had read several books about Richard Feynman when I brought one of them, a charming, touching book by Ralph Leighton, called *Tuva or Bust*, to Gordon Davidson at the Mark Taper Forum in Los Angeles. I wondered if he thought we might be able to make a play about Feynman. He thought maybe we could, and suggested that Peter Parnell write it. Peter had just written a stage version of *The Cider House Rules* and it was a thrilling piece of writing. We all decided we would try to figure out how to do a play about Feynman and the three of us started off on a journey to find out who he actually was. We thought we'd open the play a year or so later. Instead, it took us over six years.

We had no idea how hard it would be. For one thing, Feynman was an extremely unusual person. Toward the end of his life, he knew he was dying and he knew exactly what the most important questions were, and he knew he had a shot at answering them . . . and yet he kept to his habit of doing only what interested him.

He spent a good part of his time trying to get to this little place in the middle of Asia called Tuva, mainly because its capital was spelled with no vowels, which, for some reason, he found *extremely* interesting.

But, just as getting to Tuva was tantalizingly difficult for Feynman, getting to Feynman became maddeningly hard for us.

What part of him do you focus on? He helped create the atomic bomb, he helped figure out why the Challenger blew up, he understood the most puzzling questions in physics so deeply they gave him the Nobel Prize. Which facet of him do you let catch the most light? The one who was a revered teacher, a bongo player, an artist, a hilarious raconteur, or a safecracker?

We wanted to make a play about Feynman, but *which* Feynman?

A mathematician friend of mine suggested that a central image for a play about him could be Feynman's own idea of a sum over histories. Just as Feynman saw a photon taking every possible path on its way to your eye, Feynman himself took every possible path on his way through life. He was the sum of *all* his histories.

Well, nature may be smart enough to know how to average all the paths of a photon. But we three theater people couldn't figure out how to add up all the histories that made up Feynman.

At one point, I said, "You know what we ought to do? We ought to write a play about three guys sitting around in a hotel room, trying to figure out a play about Feynman. They never figure it out. They just drive themselves crazy."

We researched him like mad, of course. The people who knew him and worked with him and loved him at Caltech opened their doors and their hearts to us. They were extremely generous and helpful, as we struggled to reduce this irreducible person to an evening in the theater.

I think one of the things I most hoped would come through was his honesty. He never wanted to deceive anyone, especially himself. He questioned his every assumption. And when he was talking to ordinary people with no training in physics, he never fell back on his authority as a great thinker. He felt that if he couldn't say it in everyday words, he probably didn't understand it himself.

I was fascinated by this in him. He knew more than most of us will ever know, and yet he insisted on speaking our language.

Like Dante in his time, he could say the most exquisitely subtle things in the language of the common people. He was an American genius, and like many American artists, he was direct and colloquial…not afraid to take a look at the ordinary, and not afraid to go deeply into it to reveal the extraordinary roots of ordinary things.

And yet, he recoiled from oversimplification. He wasn't interested in dumbing down science…he was looking for clarity.

If he left something out, he always told you what he was leaving out, so you didn't get a false picture of a simplicity that wasn't there. And later, when things got more complex, you were prepared for it. He treated you, in other words, with respect.

But there was something else about him that fascinates me.

Toward the end of the New York run of QED, I was reading a book by Freeman Dyson and a paragraph about Feynman jumped off the page at me.

"Dick was…a profoundly original scientist. He refused to take anybody's word for anything. This meant that he was forced to rediscover or reinvent for himself almost the whole of physics …

He said that he couldn't understand the official version of quantum mechanics that was taught in textbooks, and so he had to begin afresh from the beginning …

At the end he had a version of quantum mechanics that he could understand."

I think I saw something in this paragraph for the first time; something suddenly clicked into place. The fact that he wouldn't take anybody's word for anything wasn't new to me, or that he needed to go through every step himself in order to understand it. A phrase of his has been on the blackboard behind me every night as I've played Feynman: "What I cannot create, I do not understand."

(People have asked us why that phrase is given so much prominence in the play. It's because the blackboard on our set contains pretty much everything that was on the final blackboard left by Feynman in his office when he died. And "What I cannot create, I do not understand" was right up there at the top.)

But what did jump out at me the other day was the phrase "he couldn't understand the official version of quantum mechanics that was taught in textbooks." Now, this is Feynman we're talking about. I suddenly had this picture in my head of Feynman going through the same experience the rest of us do …meeting that same blank wall half way up the mountain. I wondered, did that give him the ability to remember what it was like to start that climb?

So, maybe it wasn't just that he could visualize these little particles and their interactions that made him able to communicate it to the rest of us, maybe it was also that he could remember what it was like to feel dumb. Maybe he was able to make unspeakably difficult things clearer to us because he knew how hard it is for most of us to know we don't know. We often cling to our ignorance like a security blanket. We don't like uncertainty and we usually don't wander too far past the borders of the known before we gravitate back to the last comfortable view of reality we had—no matter how cockeyed it is.

But Feynman was comfortable with not knowing. He enjoyed it. He would often move forward with an idea as if he believed it was the answer. But that was only a temporary belief in order to allow himself to follow it wherever it led. Then, a little while later, he would vigorously attack the idea to see if it could stand up to every test he could think of. If it couldn't stand up, then he simply decided he just didn't know. "Not knowing," he said, "is much more interesting than believing an answer which might be wrong."

The excitement of working out a puzzle held an enormous attraction for him—no matter how many wrong turns you took on the way, and whether or not there were practical applications. To understand more about Nature was what intoxicated him. Pure science was pure pleasure. It was fun.

It's like the story of the plate.

The one thing I was certain of from the beginning was that we had to have the story of the plate in the play. It was central. Peter Parnell would do draft after draft. And I would look at it and say, "Where's the plate?" I drove him crazy.

He finally found the perfect place for the plate, as you'll see when you read the play. It was a moment in Feynman's life when he made up his mind never to work on anything that didn't interest him, that wasn't fun.

Of course, what Feynman was looking for was serious fun. It was the awe he felt when he looked at nature. And not just the official great wonders of nature, but any little part of nature, because any little part of it is as amazing and beautiful and complicated as the whole thing is. And, somehow, he was able to communicate to the rest of us, not only the wonder of it, but some understanding of the thing itself. And I still don't fully get how he did it.

Now, here's why I'm going on about this. It may not seem important how Feynman did it. Maybe we should just be glad he could do it and let it go at that. But I think it *is* important. Because, there never was a time when communicating science was as urgently needed as it is now, when massive means of destruction are right here in our hands. We're probably the first species capable of doing this much damage to our planet. We can make the birds stop singing; we can still the fish and make the insects fall from the trees like black rain. And ironically we've been brought here by reason, by rationality. We cannot afford to live in a culture that doesn't use the power in its hands with the kind of rationality that produced it in the first place.

But, just when we need rationality most, we find ourselves in a culture that increasingly holds that science is just another belief.

So, finding out who Feynman truly was—and how he made the unsayable sayable—would have been pretty nifty.

But here I am, seven years later. And, just as Feynman never got to see Tuva, I never really found Feynman. Not really. I came close, but he was too many things. He had too many histories.

Playing *QED* was immensely satisfying. It was beautifully written and beautifully directed and it gave the audience a Feynman that was as close an approximation as we could all come up with. But part of me feels that a large chunk of the man is still beyond our reach—probably beyond the reach of anyone. He's just out of sight, smiling at us. Laughing at how he put one over on us, letting us think he was just an ordinary guy. A guy we could *get*.

It turns out, though, that the old thing about the destination not being as valuable as the journey really is true.

Because, when we began our journey, *finding* Feynman seemed important, and I guess it was … but as it turned out, *looking* for Feynman has been the fun.

"He has lifted a corner of the veil of Nature."

— Einstein, writing about Louis de Broglie

"I have been trying to dance with and woo Nature all my life… but she doesn't let you lift her veil…"

— Feynman, a month before his death

CHARACTERS:
RICHARD FEYNMAN, a physicist
MIRIAM FIELD, a student

PLACE:
FEYNMAN's office at Caltech.

TIME:
ACT ONE:

A Saturday afternoon in June, 1986

ACT TWO:

That night

ACT ONE

FEYNMAN's office at Caltech.
A small outer office for his secretary.
In his actual office, a mess of books, notes, drawings,
diagrams, equations on a blackboard.
The sentence "What I cannot create, I do not understand"
is written on the blackboard.
A Saturday afternoon in June, 1986.
As the lights rise, the stage is empty for a moment.
Drumming is heard, off.

FEYNMAN
(Singing and drumming:) "There is nothing like a dame… nothing in the world…
There is nothing you can name, that is anything like a…

> *He comes through the front door.*

…Dame!"

> *He sees he is alone.*

Helen…?

> *He goes into his inner office.*

Helen!

> *He goes to his desk.*

No note. No message. You'd think she'd be here. Unless it's Saturday. Is it
Saturday?

> *He picks up the phone.*
> *He dials.*

Hello? Helen? Is it Saturday?… I figured… No, no reason, it's just, I'm… Yeah, I'm
fine… I feel good! I'm gonna work here for a while… What lecture? Oh, for the
Huntington Library? What's the subject?… "What We Know"?… Oh, I
completely forgot!… When do I have to give it? Monday?… I better work on it
today… The show? It opens Saturday. So if today is Saturday… Yeah, I'm the
Chief!… The Chief of Bali Ha'i!… Sure I'm great, I don't know why Shirley didn't
cast me as Bloody Mary!… Yeah, I could do it with a wig and a dress!… Who?
Dr. Hackett? Yeah, he's been trying to reach me. Wait. Maybe he left a message…

> *He listens to the phone messages.*

FEMALE VOICE

Professor Feynman, it's Nora Bell calling…? I'm in your Introduction to Physics class…? I have a question about chemical reactions…?

He clicks to the next message.

FEMALE VOICE #2

Mr. Feynman. My name is Nilou, we met at that exhibition of ancient Mayan hieroglyphics…

FEMALE VOICE #3

Hiya, Dick. It's Kathy. I can model for you an extra night this week.

FEMALE VOICE #4

Hello…? Uh… This is Miriam Field… I'm in your Physics X class. I have a question. I thought I'd come by today…

Click.
He picks up the phone.

FEYNMAN

These women are driving me crazy! There's no message from Hackett. See if you can track him down and have him call me here… The lecture? Yeah, I'll do it, I promise!

He hangs up.

I come in here to work on quark jets, and to practice my drumming in peace and quiet, and I get saddled with this! That's what I get for calling Helen!

FEYNMAN picks up a pad.

(*To audience:*) The thing about giving a speech like this, on "What We Know" or some such, is that nobody really wants to think about what I'm saying to begin with. Most people who go to a physics lecture know they're not going to understand it, but maybe the lecturer's going to be wearing a nice print tie they can look at.

With me, they're going to be out of luck!

What is this prejudice people have against science?

When I won the Nobel Prize, I had to go over to Sweden to get it. At dinner with the Queen of Sweden, that thing that always happens between me and royalty happened. That thing where ice forms on the surface of their faces. She asked me what I won the Nobel Prize for, and when I said "quantum physics," she said, "Oh, we can't talk about that, because nobody understands it," and I said, "On the contrary, we know quite a lot about quantum physics, and that's why we can't talk about it. It's everything else we don't know about—like how to solve poverty, and lower crime, and stop drugs, that we can talk about!" And then the ice formed on the surface of her face…

The phone rings.

Didn't matter that I was well-dressed, cause apparently I still wasn't well-mannered!

He answers it.

Yeah?… Ralph!… How'd you find me? Gweneth tell you where I was?… Yeah, I'm fine… I came over here to work and practice, and I forgot I got a damn speech to write!… I dunno, on what we don't know, or something… No, I feel great! You want to rehearse?… Say, around six?…

He grabs his drum.

You know, as soon as we come on stage with the other natives, I think we should start drumming … No, we start out with *ya de de da, ya de de da ya de de da boom!* and speed it up as fast as we can… Listen.

He puts the phone receiver down.
He drums.
He stops. He picks up the phone.

We'll try it!… What do you mean, the Russians are coming?… That's this weekend?!… You're going to the airport now?! So this is Lamin, and Lebedev, and what about Vainshtein?… Okay, yeah, after they land, take them to the hotel, and I'll see them later… Wait a minute, why don't you get them tickets for the show tonight? They'd love *South Pacific!* Good… Okay… Bye…

He hangs up.

What's the best thing about having a walk-on part? Stealing the scene! In these shows we do here at Caltech, I played one of Nathan Detroit's gamblers in *Guys & Dolls*. And the King of Sewers in *The Madwoman of Chaillot*. And last year, I played a janitor in *How To Succeed in Business Without Really Trying*. I was supposed to walk on the stage and clean things up with a broom, okay?

He grabs a makeshift shaman stick.

I have on this janitor's costume. So I pick up a wastebasket, and clean up with the broom. Then I pick up a vase with some flowers still in it, and dump it in the wastebasket. Finally, on my way out, I pick up *another* wastebasket, dump it into the first wastebasket, and leave.

Brings down the house!

And now the Russians are going to get to see me play the Chief of Bali Ha'i!

Oh! The reason the Russians are coming is that about ten years ago, Ralph and I and my wife Gweneth were playing a game of Geography one night. You know the game. You have to think of a country whose first letter is the same as the last letter of the country somebody else just said. Like I say Brazil and you say Lichtenstein. So out of the blue, I turn to Ralph—I like to kid around with him, you know—and I say, "So you think you know every country in the world, huh?" And Ralph says, "Oh, sure." And I say, "Okay, then whatever happened to Tannu Tuva?" I had remembered this country because when I was a kid, I used to collect stamps—Wait, I think I still have, right here…

He goes to an old box.

…my old stamp book.

He takes out the stamp book.

…and my favorites were these wonderfully shaped unusual stamps that came from a place just north of Mongolia, in the center of Asia, called Tannu Tuva.

And of course, not being a stamp collector himself, Ralph didn't even know where Tannu Tuva was, let alone what happened to it. So we look it up in the *Encyclopedia Brittanica*, and find it on the map. It doesn't exist anymore, technically. It's been swallowed up by the USSR. And then we see that its capital is called Kyzyl. And I think—any place that's spelled K-Y-Z-Y-L has just *got* to be in-ter-est-ing! So we decide to go!

Easier said than done.

How the heck do you get to Tuva, when no Westerner in over fifty years has gotten to go there?!

And we start to research it, and we find it's got everything, it's like Shangri-la! Lamas! Shamans! Throat singers! Throat-singing, that's—

He goes to the tape player.
He turns it on.

Throat-singing. That is one voice singing two notes at the same time. Incredible, isn't it? How do they *do* that?

And they got yaks. And yurts. Lots and lots of yurts.

So. We start reading everything about Tuva that we can. Understand. We decide we want to go to Tuva, but we want to get there like ordinary people, not like the moderately famous person I am. Besides, if the Russians knew that I, a theoretical physicist who had worked on the atomic bomb, wanted to go to Tuva, they'd probably watch me like a hawk, insist that I meet with Russian scientists, talk highfalutin' physics, the works.

Forget that!

I don't like the official way of doing anything. I don't like clubs, either. Or prizes. I get this from my father, who was a uniform salesman. He'd say to me, "You know what the difference is between a man with epaulettes and without epaulettes? *None! It's the same man!*"

One day we find this Russian-Tuvan-Mongolian phrasebook, and we start to learn Tuvan.

He has found the Tuvan phrasebook and is looking through it.

Ujur-Ash-kan-uvus-ka. Oorup tur men.

Met. Having. Our. At. Happy Am I.

So we realize English seems to be written backwards in relation to Tuvan.

Tuva-da choruva-bolur-be?

Tuva. To. Get. To. Possible. Is?

So we have this dictionary, and meanwhile we're not getting anywhere through the embassies that we're contacting, so we decide to write a letter—in Tuvan!— to the address on the back of the dictionary.

And a year later, somebody writes back!

He finds the letter in the book itself and opens it.

"Ekii, Richard Feynman and Ralph Leighton!"

Ekii means hello.

"I Daryma Ondar called I…"

His name is Ondar Daryma.

"I forty-five snowy I…"

Snowy? See we figure out that means he's forty-five years old—he's lived through forty-five winters!

"Your written having letter your reading acquainted I. Tuva in written having your gladness full am I. I this institute in Tuva folk mouth collect writing am I."

He's a folklorist who is writing a new collection of Tuvan folktales!

He sent some to us!

He looks around his desk.

I can never find anything.

The phone rings.
He answers it.

Yeah?… Danny!… Hi!… (*To audience:*) This'll just be a minute… (*On phone:*) Yeah! I'm fine! I got out about six weeks ago! I was on the table for fourteen hours! No, what happened, they opened me up to do the surgery, and then, when they were finishing, an artery close to my heart burst! I needed eighty pints of blood! Yeah, so the students here donated it! Isn't that great?!… Yeah, I'm okay… Still waiting on some tests… Oh, you saw that—Yeah, all over the papers. Yeah, the great Richard Feynman! A lot of good it did. They got my picture, supposedly solving the Challenger business. And now they won't use my report. If I have to, I'll take my name off the damn thing… Yeah? You bet I'm a pain in the ass. Hey, that's my contribution! That's why I like working with you—you do so many things that I can point out to you that are wrong… Why? What's the matter? The evolution program? No. That's not wrong. Why don't you send it to me over the computer? Yeah, we're taking the right approach. No, we're right. I did the equation. I got it right here…

He searches.

If I can just *find* the damn…

He finds something.

"The Story of the Wood Grouse and the Drake"… Hold onto that…

All right, look, let's recalculate it… C'mon, let's figure it out. No, no, c'mon, we'll do it right now. Let's do it with a Fokker-Planck equation. Okay, you use your computer.

He scribbles.

Tell me when you've stated the problem.

He puts the phone down.
He continues to scribble.
As he works:

This is a thing… my friend Danny and I are doing… that involves a giant parallel computer he's built, which itself is made up of about 65,000 tiny computers inside it! All connected by one big communications network! It actually started out as the dopiest idea I ever heard! Who could figure out such a thing?

But we did it, we're doing it, and we actually got a name for it—the Connection Machine!

He picks up the phone.

Okay, what do you got?… That's all? All you did was enter it?… I just solved it. I told you, we're right… You know, your computer's a little slow. See ya, pal.

He hangs up.
He looks at the computer.

This particular project simulates in the computer the evolution of sexually reproducing creatures over hundreds of thousands of generations! It's coming up now…

Wow. The fitness of the population makes progress in sudden leaps. Get it? *Not* by steady improvement. This duplicates the fossil record, which shows evidence that real biological evolution also exhibits something called punctuated equilibrium.

So our next step is going to be to look more closely at why this is happening. Fascinating!

See, this is just one piece in this giant puzzle, this constant attempt we go through to describe nature.

Which is a great way for me to start my lecture. "What We Know."

All of science is about trying to describe nature—whether it's biology or the known laws of physics. See, Nature is always out there, she's always doing what she does, and it's our job to try and trick her into revealing her secrets to us. It's a dance, because Nature doesn't always give up her secrets easily. You have to look closely at her; you have to experiment to really find out how she actually behaves!

He jumps up to the blackboard.

For instance, you think that light coming at you is travelling in a straight path, right?

He draws a diagram.

Here's the surface of a mirror. Here's a ray of light. Common sense tells us that the angle at which the light hits the surface is equal to the angle at which it leaves the surface, and *therefore* the light travels from its source in a path that takes the least time to get to your eye.

And not only common sense tells you this. Schoolbook physics! This is what they teach!

But it's wrong! Well, not wrong. It's true, but it's not the *whole* truth!

Or take this ball.

He throws it out to the audience.

Nice catch!

If we know the amount of time it took for that ball to travel, and do some other calculations, we can determine the path it took—there's only *one* path, the one you just saw!

But if we were in the quantum world, the world of the very tiny, and that ball were the size of an atom, or a photon of light—something *else* would be going on!

Because the behavior of things on a very tiny scale is simply different. When we get down to the world of the very small, to the particles that make up light and matter, that world behaves like nothing you've ever seen before!

Now this is not just an interesting question. In a way, this is *the* question.

If all of scientific knowledge were destroyed, and we had only one sentence that we could pass on to the next generation, what do you think that sentence would be?

I believe it is the fact that all things are made of atoms. Little particles that move around in constant motion, attracting each other when they are a little distance apart, but repelling when being squeezed into one another! Okay? But if all of life, if a stream of water, can be nothing but a pile of atoms, then I ask you an even more in-ter-est-ing question: "How much more is possible?"

Is it possible that this "thing" walking back and forth in front of you, talking to you, raising and lowering his chalk, is a great glob of these atoms in a very complex arrangement, such that the sheer complexity of it staggers the imagination as to what it can do?

Know that when we say we are a pile of atoms, we do not mean that we are *merely* a pile of atoms, but a pile of atoms which might well have the possibilities which you see standing before you!

There is a knock at the door.

WOMAN'S VOICE (*Off*)
Hello?

FEYNMAN
Yeah?

WOMAN'S VOICE (*Off*)
Professor?

FEYNMAN
Yeah?

WOMAN'S VOICE (*Off*)
Can I come in?

FEYNMAN
Sure, but I'm afraid not right now. The thing is, I'm working.

WOMAN'S VOICE (*Off*)

I'm sorry. I called earlier. Miriam Field? I'm in your Physics X class?

FEYNMAN goes to the door.

FEYNMAN

Oh, Miss Field! Right! Good name for a physicist!

FIELD (*Off*)

Thanks. But I'm not a physicist.

FEYNMAN

I know. Did you talk to my secretary? Did she call you back?

FIELD (*Off*)

Yes. I talked to her.

FEYNMAN

Good. And what did she tell you?

FIELD (*Off*)

She told me you couldn't see me today.

FEYNMAN

Right! Why don't you make an appointment with her for next week?

FIELD (*Off*)

Okay. I'll do that.

FEYNMAN

Good. Thank you. Bye.

FIELD (*Off*)

Bye.

Pause.

FEYNMAN

Hello?

FIELD

Hello?

FEYNMAN

Miss Field?

FIELD (*Off*)

Miriam.

FEYNMAN

Miriam. You're still there?

FIELD (*Off*)

Uh-huh.

FEYNMAN

Is there anything else?

FIELD (*Off*)

Can I talk to you?

FEYNMAN

You *are* talking to me.

FIELD (*Off*)

No, I mean. Can I talk to you *in person??*

FEYNMAN

You are talking to me in person!

FIELD (*Off*)

The thing is, I had this idea. I was thinking about something you said in class the other day. About some stuff you were working on. About quarks.

FEYNMAN

Quarks? Yeah?

FIELD

About the forces that bind quarks together.

FEYNMAN

Uh-huh?

FIELD

And I was wondering if you could try and solve it the way you solved QED years ago, which, according to what you said, you did by using path integrals to incorporate quantum mechanics.

FEYNMAN

Gee, that is a very in-ter-est-ing question, Miss Field.

FIELD

It is?

FEYNMAN

Yeah. Unfortunately, as an approach, it's completely wrong! Well, not wrong— it's right in principle, but incredibly difficult to do in practice!

He pulls a chair up to the door. Sits.

And it's a problem, because today we know things we didn't know then.

FEYNMAN gets up, goes to the board, and draws a picture of QED.

See, in QED, the electrons have a charge, and they create a field. We've got a positron. We've got an electron. And the field goes from the positive charge to the negative charge. But the field itself doesn't have a charge. So it spreads out over all space. (*He draws a diagram of QCD on the board.*) But when we're talking about the strong force, as in quantum chromodynamics, the gluon field *does* have a charge! So it interacts with itself, and that makes things much harder!

FIELD (*Off*)

Professor?

FEYNMAN

Yeah?

FIELD (*Off*)

Shouldn't I be *in* the room for this?

FEYNMAN

Yeah! But I still gotta—I gotta finish this lecture!

FIELD (*Off*)

You're writing a lecture?

FEYNMAN

Yeah.

FIELD (*Off*)

What's it about?

FEYNMAN

A lot. "What We Know." I'll tell you what. Why don't you come back later?

FIELD (*Off*)

Soon later or later later?

FEYNMAN

Forty-five minutes or so?

FIELD (*Off*)

How about half an hour?

FEYNMAN

Fine! Great!

FIELD is heard leaving.
Pause.

(To audience:) I really do like talking to students like in my Physics X class. Which gets all kinds of interesting people. And the ones I find the most interesting are usually the ones who don't play by the rules. I like the ones who are trying to get away with something.

When I was growing up, I was always getting myself into pickles. I was always trying to save myself.

I was in this philosophy course taught by this old bearded professor who always mumbled. I would go to class, and he would mumble along, and I couldn't understand a *thing.* I happened to have a small drill, about one-sixteenth inch, and to pass the time I would twist it between my fingers and drill holes in the sole of my shoe, week after week.

Finally one day, the Professor went "wugga mugga mugga wugga wugga" and everybody got excited! They were all talking to each other and discussing, so I figured he'd said something interesting, thank God! I wondered what it was?

I asked somebody, and he said, "We have to write a theme, and hand it in in four weeks…" "A theme on what?" "On what he's been talking about all year…" I was stuck. The only thing I could remember from the entire term was a moment where he said something about "muggawuggastreamofconsciousnessmuggawugga" and *phoom!* It sank back into chaos.

This stream of consciousness idea reminded me of a problem my father had given to me many years before.

Suppose you're a Martian, he said to me, and you come down to earth, and Martians never sleep. Suppose you don't even know what sleep *is*. So you ask, how does it *feel* to go to sleep? What *happens?* Do your thoughts suddenly stop, or do they move less annndd leesss rrraaaaappppiidddddlllyyy?

I got interested. How does the stream of consciousness *end* when you go to sleep? So every afternoon for the next few weeks I would work on my theme. I would pull down the shades in my room, turn off the lights, and go to sleep. And I'd watch what *happened.*

At first I noticed a lot of things that had little to do with falling asleep. I noticed that I did a lot of thinking by speaking to myself internally. I could also imagine things visually.

Then, when I was getting tired, I noticed that I could think of two things at once. The thoughts become more and more cockeyed and disjointed, and beyond that, you fall asleep…

After four weeks of sleeping all the time, I wrote my theme. I ended it with a little verse I made up.

I wonder why. I wonder why.
I wonder why I wonder.
I wonder *why* I wonder why.
I wonder why I wonder!

We hand in our themes, and the next time our class meets, the professor reads one of them:

"Mum bum wugga mum bum…"

Then another:

"Mugga wugga mum bum wugga…"

Then another:

"Uh wugga wuh. Uh wugga wuh.
Uh wugga wugga wugga.
Uh wugga *wuh* uh wugga wuh.
Uh wugga wugga wugga."

Aha! That's my theme! I had saved myself again!

> *He runs to his notepad.*
> *He writes.*

This is good. I can also put this in my lecture. About "What We Know"!

> *The phone rings.*
> *FEYNMAN looks at it.*
> *He lets the machine pick it up.*

MACHINE
Dick Feynman here.

HACKETT'S VOICE
Dick, it's Dr. David Hackett, calling you back. Helen told me you were in your office…

> *FEYNMAN picks it up.*

FEYNMAN
Yeah?… Doc! I got your message… I feel pretty good, yeah!… I had some dizziness last night… Not so much, a little while I was jogging… The prednisone? Yeah, I take that pill every day. I take it without fail.

> *He downs the pill with water.*

What's the matter?… Are you sure?… On the CT scan?… How large?… Larger than the last time? Well, that doesn't sound too good… Where is it? I see… When would you want me to go back into the hospital?… Monday? Why so soon?

Yeah, I understand, but I'm thinking, what about trying to *shrink* the tumor? Maybe I should talk to the oncologist… Okay, I'll—Yeah, I'll give him a call, and call you back…

He hangs up.

This cancer I've got is the oddest thing—it doesn't metastasize! It just spreads. It just grows out from one place, like a giant tree.

He picks up the phone.

The first cancer I got, in my abdomen, got removed about four years ago along with one of my kidneys. They thought they got it all. Then it showed up in a crazy pattern around my intestines. Dr. Hackett told me he wanted to cut out as much of it as he possibly could. He said he wouldn't stop until he saw the operating table underneath.

He's a great surgeon, but folks go to him as a last resort. I mean, as surgeons go, he's a real cowboy!

He dials.

Hackett told me he never expected me to make it through that first surgery—and I've had two more since!

Hello? Is Dr. Thornton there?… He's out?… What's your name?… Carl?… I have a son named Carl!… How old are you?… Ten?… Wow, you're old… Yeah, my son Carl is a little older than you… He was ten almost twelve years ago… You know how old that makes him?… What's twelve plus ten, Carl?… Very good… Is your mama there?… Sure…

He is holding.

In the hospital the last time, when I was recovering, I had a pretty good time. What I'd do, I'd get up while the doctors weren't looking, and secretly read my chart. Then, when the doctors came by, they'd say, "How are you feeling, Professor?" And I'd say, "I think okay, but I feel like my blood pressure is up about three points today…" And they'd say, "That's amazing, Dr. Feynman! How did you know that?!"

(*On phone:*) Yeah… Hello, this is Dick Feynman… Hi, Mrs. Thornton… Yeah, if he could call me when he gets back from the hospital… I'll give you my office number. 81… Okay, sure, go ahead…

He is holding.

I also got this rare blood thing called Waldenstrom's macro-globulinemia. It's in the bone marrow. A B lymphocyte, a white blood cell, is producing too much of a certain protein. So they've started me on chemotherapy in this rotten pill form...

Yeah, I'm still here, take your time...

Plus, I got this arrhythmia. My father had it. I had an attack while Ralph and I were up at Esalen last year, and some hippie doctor gave me tons of fizzy soda pop to drink. We were on our way back to Pasadena, and I suddenly burped louder than I had ever burped before, and my heartbeat went back to normal. So we turned around and headed right back to the hot tubs!

Yeah, I'm in Pasadena... 626-395-8882... Okay... Thank you!

> *He hangs up.*
> *Pause.*

I gotta tell you, I hate the idea of going back to the hospital!

> *The phone rings.*
> *He picks up.*

Yeah?... Gweneth!... I thought maybe it was the oncologist... Yeah, Hackett found me... He thinks the sarcoma's back again... A tumor, yeah... wrapped around the other kidney... He doesn't know how big... Pretty big I think, but... Well, yeah, he wants to go back in... He said pretty soon, but I'm waiting to hear back from Thornton. Sure, after the show tonight, we can talk it over... No, you don't need to, darling... I'll see you later! Love you!

> *He hangs up.*
> *Pause.*

I'm sure she can take the news, but I don't like to worry her. You could get emotional about something like this.

The thing about solving a problem—in science or in life—about letting yourself think like a Martian a little, is that you have to think a problem through rationally, even if you disagree with your outcome emotionally. See, if your intuition doesn't accept what your reasoning concludes, that's okay—you're entitled to your feelings. But at least you've gotten yourself to *think* about it!

At Los Alamos, we were under tremendous pressure; we were racing against Hitler to build the bomb. And to alleviate the pressure—to help myself think clearly—I did two things—I played the drums, and I broke into the safes!

I had learned how to pick locks from a guy named Leo Lavetelli. What I love about locks is, it's a puzzle—one guy tries to make something to keep another guy out. There must be a way to beat it.

I learned how locks worked. Then I studied combination locks and learned how to pick off certain numbers. I practiced all the time on my own safe. At Los Alamos, all the secrets of the project were kept in filing cabinets which, if they had locks at all, were locked with padlocks that had maybe only three pins: they were easy as pie to open. Later they got newer cabinets, and I got good at those, too.

Whenever you read these books written by safecrackers—there are these books by safecrackers—they always have introductions like, "I cracked the safes for the greatest heist in history!" or, " I picked the lock and saved the girl!" But if I wrote a safecracker book, my introduction would be the best one of all. Because I managed to open the safes that contained all the secrets to the atomic bomb! *The whole schmeer!* It took me about a year and a half to do it! But, of course, I was *building* the bomb, too!

The phone rings.

Yeah?… Oh! Mr. Chairman!… I thought you were a doctor actually… Yeah, I'm fine! I'm great!… A bad time? No, right now is… it's okay…

Yeah… I've read the report…

He fishes around in the desk.

I think we should drop the tenth recommendation from our conclusion. It's not that I disagree with it. It's that I think it's inappropriate.

He finds the statement.
He reads aloud.

Look what it says. "The Commission strongly recommends that NASA continue to receive the support of the Administration and the nation *blah blah blah* symbol of national pride, uh… The Commission applauds NASA's spectacular achievements—" Mr. Chairman, between you and me and the rest of the country this is *exactly* the kind of BS that I simply won't—

He throws the paper down.

We're filing a report about an accident that resulted in a national tragedy! It's inappropriate because it's a policy statement... I *know* it prevents us from sounding too critical! *That's the problem!* We *must* be critical! ... What do you mean, I've been outvoted?! How was I outvoted when there was no meeting?... *I know* I was in the hospital! That doesn't mean I couldn't vote!... Sure, I'm angry! No, I'm not going to agree with anything right now! In fact, I'll take my name off the report entirely!... Goodbye.

He hangs up.

How do you like that?!

If that isn't one of the most—Here I am, I give up six months of my *life*—There's this Presidential Commission, they beg me to come to Washington, they want me to help figure out what happened to the space shuttle Challenger. There was one good guy there, a General Kutyna, and he told me, he said, "Everybody on this thing is too inside, you're the only one who can do anything"—only, always check six o'clock! It's an airforce term. You're flying along, everything looks clear in front of you and on the sides, but you forget to check *behind* you! In other words, *watch your back!*

And it was Kutyna who mentioned the effect of cold on the O-rings to me. He was the guy who first turned me on to the fact that the cold had made the O-rings lose their elasticity. And the day I demonstrated it by putting the rubber O-ring in the ice water, he's the guy who whispered to me when to do it, how to get the cameras on me.

The damn thing blew up. It was a tragic mistake. The managers tried to violate a simple law of nature. And the engineers, the guys underneath, knew it... but there was a problem, somehow the word didn't get to the top.

At Los Alamos, we knew there were tremendous risks and we tried to do something about it.

I had gone to Los Alamos because Bob Wilson at Princeton cornered me. He suggested that my intelligence, arrogance, and general unwillingness to accept authority might come in handy.

He was right!

So I went out there, with my first wife, Arlene, who was ill with tuberculosis. We put her in a sanitarium in Albuquerque. And I would travel every weekend from Los Alamos to see her.

But that's another story.

Anyway. There was a plant in Oak Ridge, Tennessee that was where they were actually trying to separate the isotopes of uranium—U 238 and U 235, the explosive one. The people in Oak Ridge didn't know anything about what it was to be used for, they didn't know how powerful the bomb was, or how it worked or anything. And the people on top wanted to keep it that way. But it was very dangerous, and they had not paid any attention to the safety at all!

So Oppenheimer comes to me and says, "There's going to be a meeting down there, and I want you to go to that meeting and tell them what the dangers are. You tell them, 'Los Alamos cannot accept the responsibility for the safety of the Oak Ridge plant unless etc., etc…'"

I was twenty-five years old. And I say, "You mean, me, little Richard, is going to go in and say that?"

And Oppenheimer says, "Yes, you, little Richard, are going to go in and do that!"

So I go down there, and I talk to this one Lieutenant, and he goes and talks to this Colonel, and then the Colonel goes and talks to this General. And then the General comes and talks to *me*.

I tell him, "Los Alamos cannot accept the responsibility for the safety of the Oak Ridge plant unless …"

And the General says, "Just five minutes," and then he goes to a window and stands there and thinks. That's what they're good at, these military guys— making decisions. And sure enough, five minutes later, he comes back and says, "All right, Mr. Feynman, go ahead!"

I was amazed—because I can never make up my mind about anything of any importance in any length of time at all!

The phone rings.
FEYNMAN lets it ring.

MACHINE

Dick Feynman here.

RALPH'S VOICE

Chief! Pick up the phone. The plane's in, I'm here at the airport…

FEYNMAN picks up.

FEYNMAN

Ralph! I was just thinking—in the new book—I think we should try and find a place for the Challenger business… Yeah… So the Russians have arrived? Is that them singing?… No, no, don't…

He waits.
Then, in Russian:

Strazvuityeh! Dobroh podjalovat ve America! Kak ve doletyeli? Horosho, horosho!… Segodnia vecherom vi uvidyete menia I Ralpha in our show. Eto a musical. It'll make you smeyatsia I plakat.

These guys sound like they're completely drunk on their ass.

Tomorrow, poydiem our exhibit. Potom v Disneyland, I Micki Mouse! Da! Get some sleep!

He hangs up.

It's incredible that these Russians are actually here! And all because Ralph and I—

Oh! The whole *point* of my starting to tell you before about how our trying to get to Tuva—

One day Ralph comes to me, all excited. He'd found this book, called *Nomads of Siberia*, written by this Professor Vainshtein, a Russian who is an expert on Tuvan archaeology. And we find out that this guy is excavating Tuvan artifacts for an exhibition on nomads of Eurasia.

So Ralph goes to Moscow to see this Vainshtein, and he comes back with a great idea: *We* would help Vainshtein's exhibit come to America! This would all be done through unofficial channels, of course—because Vainshtein and these other two guys knew I was a physicist. And we'd arrange with a film company for us to go *to* Tuva to do a documentary about the whole thing! We'd be art curators! And movie makers!

And now the exhibit has come here! To the LA Natural History Museum! And so have the Russians! It's all moving forward, except we haven't done *our* part yet—we haven't found a movie company willing to go along with it! Who knows if we will? The movie business is crazier than the Tuvan artifact business! Our timing is going to have to be right!

He goes to a chair and sits.

Timing is everything, isn't it?

"What We Know"…

So you see, in physics we're always trying to figure out what we don't understand about nature. And it's very tough. It's like watching a chess game without knowing the rules, and trying to understand the rules just by watching the moves. Things can be going along well, you *think* you're getting all the laws. You might discover, for example, that one of the bishops is always on a red square. Later on, you might discover that the law for a bishop is it moves on the diagonal which would explain why it's always on red. Then all of a sudden, some strange phenomenon occurs… That bishop is suddenly on a black square! And that's because the bishop had been captured and taken off the board. And then later, a pawn had gone all the way down to the other end to produce a queen, and that bishop still looks like a bishop, but now it's standing in for a queen, and it can go anywhere. So something happens you didn't expect… Sometimes when you're trying to trick Nature into telling you her secrets, she ends up surprising you… and *that*! Suddenly *that* is the most interesting thing of all!

For instance. Light. At first it was believed that light behaves like a shower of particles. Then, with further research, it was thought it behaves like waves. Light emanating out from a source might travel like waves on water. But *then*, even later, it was decided that it actually behaves like particles *and* waves!

So which is it? Waves or particles? "Photons of light behave like waves"—no, they don't, exactly. "They act like particles"—no, they don't, exactly. Rather, photons and electrons behave in their own inimitable manner! They are both screwy, but at least they're both screwy in exactly the same way!

Look, you want to see an example of screwy? Take a surface of glass. You see me because light is coming through the glass and hitting my face, but you also see yourself because some of the light is reflecting back. At this angle, 90 degrees, for every 100 photons hitting the glass, 96 go through the glass, and 4 hit the glass and go back to you. How does any individual photon make up its mind which way to go?

Already, it's a mystery! Try as we might to explain how a photon makes up its mind, it is actually impossible to predict *which way* a given photon will go!

Does this mean that physics, a science of great exactitude, has been reduced to calculating only the *probability* of an event, and not predicting exactly what will happen?

Yes. Nature permits us to calculate only probabilities…

The phone rings.
He lets the machine pick up.

MACHINE
Dick Feynman here.

THORNTON'S VOICE
Dr. Feynman, it's Dr. Ed Thornton calling…

CARL'S VOICE
And Carl!

FEYNMAN goes to it.

FEYNMAN
Doctor!… Thanks for calling back… You talked to Hackett?… He wants me to go in Monday… Have you looked at the CT scans? Not yet? Okay… What are the chances of shrinking the tumor?… Depending on its size, right… Oh yeah, that hyperthermia thing you were talking about. Yeah, I looked at that article you sent me last time… It sounds nuts!

He laughs.
He looks for the article.

You mean like a microwave? What good would heating it do?… And you've had some success with this?… No. I'm not saying I wouldn't try it, I just don't understand how it works. Even you say in here *you* don't understand how it works!… Yeah, I'll read about this, and you look at the CT scan, and—say goodnight to Carl…

He hangs up.
He finds the JAMA article.

This cancer stuff is so in-ter-est-ing! This guy is working on a therapy with radio waves that heat up the tumor… Only *how* does it do it?

When Arlene was sick, when we were out in New Mexico, I was working hard on the bomb, day and night, and like I told you, I'd drive to see her on weekends. And it was tough because, we knew she was very ill, but they were working on these new medicines for TB, they were experimenting with streptomycin, and it seemed as if any day now, they might come up with a cure.

The reality of the situation was very important to me. I had to know, I had to understand what was happening to Arlene's body physiologically.

He stops, remembering.

Funny. I came from a family where telling the truth was important. Arlene came from a family that was polite, telling little white lies all the time. I taught her not to care what other people think. And she really got good at it.

She used to send me pencils, from the hospital, to Los Alamos. Pencils with writing on them. "Richard darling, I love you! Putsy."

And I, I had to *use* those pencils, and for some reason, I dunno, I was embarrassed, maybe, by the emotion of it. I've always been—Anyway, I didn't want to waste the pencils, so I tried cutting the writing off them. And Arlene *knew* what I'd do—she was ahead of me! The very next day, she writes me: "What's the idea of trying to cut my name off the pencils? Aren't you proud of the fact that I love you? What do you care what other people think?!"

What *did* I care, huh? (*Laughs.*) What did I care...

I've tried hard not to care ever since.

A couple years after she died, I wrote Arlene a letter. I added a P.S. at the end of it.

"Forgive me for not mailing this, but I don't know your new address." I don't know where you are…

Pause.
There is a knock at the door.

FIELD (*Off*)

Professor? Hello?

FEYNMAN

Yeah…

FIELD (*Off*)

Hi. It's me. I'm back.

FEYNMAN

Jeez. Is it forty-five minutes already?

FIELD (*Off*)

You said half an hour.

FEYNMAN

Is it half an hour already?

FIELD (*Off*)

I may be a little early.

FEYNMAN

The thing is, I'm running a little late.

FIELD (*Off*)

Oh, I'm sorry.

FEYNMAN

It's okay.

FIELD (*Off*)

Are you all right?

FEYNMAN

Yeah. Why?

FIELD (*Off*)

I don't know. Your voice sounds a little funny. Different.

FEYNMAN

It does?

FIELD (*Off*)

You having some trouble with "What You Know"?

FEYNMAN
No. It's not that exactly.

FIELD (*Off*)
I was thinking about those quarks again.

FEYNMAN
Yeah?

FIELD (*Off*)
They really are funny little things, aren't they?

FEYNMAN
You could say that!

FIELD (*Off*)
You were talking in class the other afternoon, about the things inside the nucleus, the quarks, the gluons…

FEYNMAN
Right…

FIELD (*Off*)
And then I thought I heard you say that even when the quarks are far apart from each other, their attraction doesn't weaken.

FEYNMAN
That *is* what I said—

FIELD (Off)
Good. I wasn't sure; I'd just woken up—

FEYNMAN
Yeah, and that was unexpected because—What do you mean, you'd just woken up?

FIELD (*Off*)
I don't know. I'd drifted off, I guess. To sleep.

Pause.

FEYNMAN
(*Laughs.*) I like your style, Miss Field.

(*Laughs.*) You do?

FEYNMAN

Yes!

FIELD (*Off*)

Great! Anyway. I'd better go. And Dick? Good luck with "What You Know."

FEYNMAN opens the door.

FEYNMAN

Miss Field?

FIELD (*Off*)

Yeah?

FEYNMAN

I'll tell you what. Why don't we talk about your questions later? After the show tonight.

FIELD (*Off*)

You mean *South Pacific*?

FEYNMAN

Yeah. At the party.

FIELD enters.

FIELD

There's a party?

FEYNMAN

After. Come and find me. I'll be wearing the chief costume. The Chief of Bali Ha'i!

FIELD

Okay. I'll see you there later.

FEYNMAN

Good. Great!

FIELD leaves.
FEYNMAN drums.

Women!

I have to be careful. I love women! *All* women! When I walk down the street, I see *only* women. The men are just fuzzy blurs.

Women are mysterious. Like Nature. In fact, I'm sure that Nature is a woman.

It's women who made me want to be an artist!

I have this friend Jerry Zorthian, who is a crazy artist. We'd have these discussions about art and science. Jerry would say, you scientists destroy the beauty of Nature. You pick it apart and turn everything into equations!

And I'd say that's ridiculous! Scientific knowledge only *adds* to the excitement and mystery and the awesomeness of a flower. Someday science is going to figure out how art is done—and *then* you boys are going to be in big trouble!

So we made a deal. I would teach Jerry science, if he would teach me how to draw.

Which I thought would be *impossible!*

Zorthian turned out to be a very good teacher. I began to work hard at it because… well, I began to want to learn how to draw for a reason I kept to myself.

FEYNMAN, who has been drumming, sags suddenly.
He stops drumming.

Sorry. I'm okay. It's just a momentary… I get this pain.

He crosses to his desk.
He writes something down.
He takes a pill.

I wanted to learn how to draw because I wanted to convey an emotion I have about the beauty of the world. It's difficult to describe because it's an emotion. It's an appreciation of the mathematical beauty of Nature, of how she works inside… It's a feeling of awe—of scientific awe… about the glories of the universe… expressed in a drawing.

Also, there were the nude models.

Most of my models I got through Zorthian, but I also tried to get models on my own. Whenever I met a young woman who looked as if she would be interesting to draw, I would ask her to pose for me. It always ended up that I would draw her face, because I didn't know exactly how to bring up the subject of posing nude.

Once when I was over at Zorthian's, I said to his wife Dabney, I can never get the girls to pose nude. I don't know how Jerry does it!

And Dabney said, "Well, did you ever *ask* them?"

Oh! I never thought of that!

I've done a lot of drawing since then, and I've gotten so I like to draw nudes best. There were topless restaurants in town. You could go there for lunch or dinner, and the girls would dance without a top, and after a while without anything. I'd sit in one of the booths drinking soda, and work a little physics on the paper placemats with the scalloped edges, and sometimes I'd draw the dancing girls, just to practice.

One of my favorite places to go was a bar called Gianonni's. One day I found out there was a police raid on Gianonni's, and some of the dancers were arrested. There was a big court case about it; it was in all the local papers.

So Gianonni goes around to every table and asks the customers if they would testify in support of him. Everybody has an excuse. "I run a day camp, and if the parents see that I'm going to this place…" or "I'm in such-and-such business, and if it's publicized that I come down here…"

I think to myself, "I'm the only free man in here. I *like* this place, and I'd like to see it continue. I don't see anything wrong with topless dancing." So I say to Gianonni, "Sure, I'll be glad to testify."

The papers have a field day. CALTECH NOBEL PRIZE WINNER ATTENDS TOPLESS BAR!

Gianonni told me I was the most respectable customer who testified for him. And he still lost the case!

I once actually got to have an exhibit. This one drawing I had was a portrait of a beautiful blonde model from art class. And I had always been interested in Madame Curie. So what happened was…

The phone rings.
He lets the machine pick up.

MACHINE

Dick Feynman here.

HACKETT'S VOICE

Dr. Feynman, it's Dr. Hackett again…

He jumps on it.

FEYNMAN

Doc!… Sorry I didn't call you back… I talked to Thornton. He hasn't looked at the CT scan yet. Decide tonight?… I thought I had a little more time than that… Well, sure, you gotta prepare for Monday…

What's the risk involved, while I'm on the table?… And what about post-operatively? You're taking into account my arrythmia?… And the blood disease? That lowers immunity, right, so we're also talking… Uh huh. Okay.

So what are my chances? 100%?! Of dying or living? Both?

He laughs.

You're giving me really crazy odds, doc! It's like you're saying, flip a coin!

I know you don't gamble, and yet, you're one of the biggest gamblers I know!…

Look, I'm going to need a little more time. To think about this. I'll call you later! After the show.

He hangs up.
FEYNMAN remains still for a moment.

What should I do? Should I do this?

How can I answer such a question?

"If I do this, what will happen?" See, that's usually a scientific question. The answer is: "Try it and see."

But with this, you don't get a second try.

I can solve this. It's another puzzle. Another lock to pick. Another safe to crack.

An in-ter-est-ing thing to figure out.

> *The timer goes off.*
> *Pause.*
> *He turns it off.*
> *He grabs his medical book.*

I got to go to the theatre! Time to put on my costume and become the Chief! Hail to the Chief! The Chief of Bali Ha'i!

> *He starts out.*
> *He stops, remembering.*

Oh! So at the exhibit I had this one drawing, a portrait of a beautiful blonde model from art class, and I called it "Madame Curie Observing the Radiations from Radium." The message I intended to convey was, nobody thinks of Madame Curie as a woman, as feminine, with beautiful hair, bare breasts, and all that. They only think of the radium part.

> *VOICES are heard, off.*

Who the hell is that…?

> *RUSSIAN VOICES singing, drunk.*

Oh, my God! It's Ralph! And the Russians! (*Calls:*) Ralph! Keep them there! Don't come in! I'm coming out!

So I'm at the exhibit and one of the art lovers comes over and starts up a conversation with me. "Tell me, do you draw from photographs or from models?" "I always draw directly from a posed model," I say to her. "Well," she says, "how did you ever get Madame Curie to pose for you?"

(*He shouts back, in Russian:*) Tovarischy dobroh pozhalovat v'Caltech!!

> *And he is out the door.*

END OF ACT ONE

ACT TWO

That night.
The office is in shadow.
Drumming is heard, off.

FEYNMAN

(*Off:*) All Hail the Chief! The Chief of Bali Ha'i!

He enters.
He is dressed in a chieftain outfit.
Robe, headdress.
He drums.

Like the headdress?

There's a tribe I've heard about in which the members of the tribe are allowed to act as crazy as they want, do whatever they want to do, whenever they put a leaf in their hair. If you do something nutty, you can always say, "Well, I had a leaf in my hair."

The Russians, by the way, had a terrific time. Turns out they love Rodgers & Hammerstein in Moscow.

At the party after, I toasted them.

He pretends to toast.

…And so you can understand how much of a delight it is for me to greet you, to see a kind of reality resulting from the nonsense which we began! Will we ever to get to Tuva? With your help, it is our profound hope that we will!

Then they all had another round of vodka.

Tonight, Bali Ha'i! Tomorrow, the Natural History Museum, and Disneyland!

Lucky buggers.

FEYNMAN turns on the lights.

Zorthian and his wife enjoyed themselves immensely. He brought along one of his models. Nifty. *Very* beautiful.

He listens to the answering machine.

ROGERS'S VOICE

Dr. Feynman, it's Bill Rogers calling again… If you get this tonight, call me here in Washington, no matter how late… I want to discuss a compromise…

FEYNMAN picks up the phone.
Dials.

FEYNMAN

Mr. Chairman?… Feynman… What kind of compromise?… I accept the tenth recommendation, you accept my own report… Wait—Except for *which* sentence?

He goes through papers.

"The Story of the Wood Grouse and the…" Good God!

He goes through more papers.
He gets back on the phone.
He reads.

Okay. Where are you?… "Official management claims to believe the probability of failure is a thousand times less…" Uh…

"Let us take steps to ensure that NASA officials deal in a world of reality…" Which sentence is too polemical?…

He reads it silently.

Okay. Maybe. Maybe it's too polemical… I'll tell you what. If I remove that sentence, then I offer *this* change on the Committee's tenth recommendation: *Don't call it a recommendation!* It sounds too important, and it's not! Make it simply a concluding thought or something.

And *my* report would end as follows: "For a successful technology, reality must take precedence over public relations, for Nature cannot be fooled…"

Why don't you think about that, okay? Right… Goodnight…

He hangs up.
Pause.
He looks at the report.

"…Nature cannot be fooled…"

It's startling, isn't it? How an extraordinary piece of equipment can be destroyed, blown to pieces in a fraction of a second… because of a tiny little thing, an O-ring. I mean, to launch in 29-degree weather without looking at performance data at low temperature—without at least trying to *quantify* uncertainty!

Startling? Yes. But surprising? Not really.

Because they forgot one of the basic rules: If you ask Nature the right question, she will give you the right answer.

> *Pause.*
> *He picks up the phone.*
> *He dials.*

Dr. Thornton? It's Feynman… Well, I took your paper with me and, during the show tonight, when I wasn't onstage, I was reading it again… You know why I think your crazy idea works? When you heat up the tumor, you stimulate its metabolic rate and it gets starved for nourishment. It's like when you run a car motor very very fast; it'll run out of gas sooner.

We got it, doc! I think we figured it out!

> *He laughs.*

Now did you look at the CT scan? Could this hyperthermia work for me?… Too big, huh?… How much could we shrink it?… Not enough time… No, I understand, if you think… It's surgery or nothing at this point… I better read about kidney function, I suppose… Well I want to find out for myself.

> *He picks up the Merck Manual.*

What about this? In the show tonight, one of the natives was played by this blood guy, a researcher. So while we were standing there waiting to go on, he was telling me about this capillary disease in children: to stop the growth of all these capillaries, he uses Alpha 2 Interferon. So I'm thinking, my tumor is loaded with capillaries. What if we try to kill them off with interferon? I mean, wouldn't that be in-ter-est-ing??

I'm trying to reinvent medicine? You bet I'm trying to reinvent it!… Yeah. Okay. Goodnight.

> *He hangs up.*

How else am I going to figure out this damn puzzle?!

He opens JAMA.

When I was a kid growing up in Far Rockaway, I loved to solve puzzles. In high school, during first period a guy would come to me with a puzzle in geometry. I wouldn't stop until I figured the damn thing out. Then, during the day, other guys would come to me with the same problem, and I'd do it for them in a flash. So for one guy, it took me twenty minutes, while there were five guys who thought I was a super-genius.

So I got a fancy reputation. And it might not have been all that deserved, but what did I care?!

Then later, at Cornell, I was *still* solving puzzles! Only they were bigger! I tried solving the infinities in quantum electrodynamics, QED. I'd worked on it since graduate school. But the thing is, I solved it my own way, by creating my own system! Because I didn't trust the experts who'd solved everything before me, I re-solved everything they did, as if it was the first time! Know How To Solve Every Problem That's Already Been Solved! That's one of my mottoes!

He points at the blackboard.

Because "What I Cannot Create, I Do Not Understand!" Look, like this.

Remember I told you that everybody says that the light reflected off a mirror travels the fastest path to your eye?

I figured out that what's *actually* happening is that every single photon is taking *every possible path*—travelling to *every* part of the mirror on its way to your eye—coming at you in all kinds of crazy angles! Here. Look at all these crazy paths. That's just one photon taking all these crazy paths at once. But most of the paths cancel each other out.

Overall, we find that Nature herself combines all the paths into one average path, and that's the path we see.

What I did was I got *inside* the electron! I put myself *in* nature! As a darting photon. As a particle of light.

He draws on the blackboard.

Here is one example of an interaction. This is time moving forward. This is space. A pair of electrons moves toward each other. Then a virtual photon is emitted by the right-hand electron and the electron is deflected outward—like when you shoot a rifle, you recoil.

The virtual photon is absorbed by the other electron, and it, too, is deflected out… like when you shoot at a tin can, the tin can goes flying!

And my way of looking at QED proved to be both a physical theory and a way of calculating that theory! I found a whole new way of looking at this stuff, by *re-in-vent-ing* it!

One night, in my pajamas, working on the floor with papers all around me, I stared at these crazy-looking diagrams, like this one right here—and I said to myself, I'm the only guy making these pictures. Everybody else uses only equations. But I need to draw it, to do a road map. Wouldn't it be funny if these diagrams really are useful, and other people start using them? And they did! And all the science journals had to print these silly pictures!

But it was so exciting! I got so caught up in solving it!

> *Pause.*
> *He looks at the medical book.*

Sometimes you get so caught up with solving a puzzle you lose sight of the reality of the world outside the puzzle.

This says that there's a high risk of losing kidney function *completely* with this operation.

It's like when we were working on the bomb. Those of us who worked on it got so involved with solving it, we forgot what it was we were solving… But it was so exciting…

I saw it go off, you know. The bomb.

I am about the only guy who actually looked at the damn thing. Everybody else was wearing the dark glasses, and the people at six miles couldn't see it because they were all told to lie on the floor.

But I was twenty miles away. You couldn't see a damn thing through dark glasses. So I figured the only thing that could really hurt your eyes is ultraviolet light. I got behind a truck windshield, because the ultraviolet can't go through glass. Time comes. There's this tremendous flash so bright that I duck, and I see this purple splotch on the floor of the truck. I think, that's not it; that's an after-image. So I look back up, and I see this white light changing into yellow and then into orange. Clouds form and disappear. Finally, the big ball of orange starts to rise and billow, and get a little black around the edges, and then you see it's a big ball of smoke with lightening flashes on the inside, the heat of the fire going outwards.

It all took about a minute.

Then about thirty seconds later, a tremendous noise. Then a rumble, like thunder… and that's what convinced me. That it had really worked.

Afterwards, we had parties. We all ran around. I sat on the hood of a jeep and beat my drum.

And one man, Bob Wilson, was just sitting there.

"What are you moping about?" I said.

He said, "It's a terrible thing that we made."

I said, "But you started it. You got us—you got me—into it."

See, that's the thing. We... we had a great time at Los Alamos. *Too* good a time. That was, that was what made Bethe say that we sinned. We sinned because we enjoyed solving the problems of the bomb. Like we would enjoy solving any big problem. And although it was started for the right reasons, it was dumb, ultimately. A dumb, stupid idea.

But you're working very hard to accomplish something, to figure it out. And it's a pleasure, it's excitement. And you stop thinking. You just *stop*.

After the War, right after coming home, I was in New York. I was sitting in a restaurant. I knew how big the bomb was, how big an area it covered. And I realized that from where I was sitting, at 59th Street, to drop such a bomb on 34th Street—the radiation would spread all the way up from Ground Zero, and all these people would be killed.

I began to measure all distances that way. From Ground Zero… through lethal radiation… all the way to fire damage. And it was amazing to me that people were going on living… writing symphonies, building bridges… as if Hiroshima had never happened.

It's senseless, I would think. Don't they all realize everything's going to be destroyed very soon…?

> *Pause.*
> *The phone rings.*
> *He picks up.*

Yeah?… Hiya, Dr. Hackett… Sorry, I know I was supposed to call you after the show. Listen, I was just reading here if I do this operation, I'll probably lose my one good kidney and be on dialysis for the rest of my life… Mmm… You know, I'm wondering, what am I looking at, if we *don't* go in?… Six months? A year?… Sure, I know you can't, I know you don't like to say… I see…

You know what? Let me call you back in a couple of minutes. Bye.

> *He hangs up.*

It's like the hundred photons hitting the glass… Am I one of the 96 that go through, or one of the 4 that bounce back? There's no way to know…

> *He picks up the phone.*
> *He dials.*

Gweneth… Hi darling. The show was great, wasn't it? No, I didn't stay long at the party… I'm at the office, yeah. I'm still trying to figure this out.

Maybe it's better to go on living my life like I have been, and make the most of the time I got left… Hackett's given me four years I wouldn't have had… It's not giving up! It's simply accepting what is!

Yeah, but why should I take the risk? He can't even tell me how much time the operation would buy me… Hope? I have to have hope?… What do you mean I have—You know that's not me!… Okay, I'll be home soon, darling.

> *He hangs up.*

Hope! Why have hope? What does hope get you?

Say you're lost, your plane's crashed, and you're in the snow, in the middle of nowhere. And you decide to walk on, to try and get help… And you walk… And your determination keeps you going… And hope? You hope you make it… But does your hope, your *faith* that you will survive… actually *help* you survive? Is there empirical evidence of this?… Maybe, after all, it would be better if you stayed with your car, or your ship… help might find you more easily. By not walking, maybe you could even live longer…

Is hope simply an illusion to maintain activity?

Is hope, then, related to fear?

Fear of what might happen? Is it fear that causes us to not look at the reality of what faces us? Fear that causes us to make myths, and believe in them? To create a heaven, for instance. Instead of calmly saying to ourselves… this is the situation…

Many people have faced death calmly… being good to themselves… and they're thinking people…

Like my father.

My father taught me how to look at things. He would see a bird, and tell me, don't worry what the bird is called. Watch what it *does*.

He finds a notebook.

These are his notes of all the birds.

Brown-throated thrush. Pecks its feathers. Pecks more when it first lands. Is it fleas?

It's in his own handwriting.

When he was sick, he knew death might come at any moment. He'd have a blind spot and try to analyze it, he'd think, a small blood vessel must have burst. That is what's happening more and more inside my brain.

He died from a stroke. At the internment, Bayside Cemetery, in Queens, the Rabbi, Rabbi Cahn asked me to say Kaddish with him.

He began.

"Yis ga dol ve yis ka dosh she may rabah…"

I listened to the words but I wouldn't repeat them.

I don't believe in God. My father didn't believe in God.

Later, my mother shouted at me, "How could you?! In front of the Rabbi?!"

Because I don't believe! He didn't believe!

Why should I console myself with crazy, mythical thinking?!

Arlene hadn't.

When she first got sick, we made a pact that we must speak honestly with each other and look at everything directly. When we thought she had Hodgkins disease—she didn't, we found out later, she had TB, but when we *thought* she did—her parents convinced me to tell her instead that she had glandular fever. I couldn't bear it, but I lied to her. She believed me, but later, when she suspected something was wrong, she asked me again.

"Richard, do I have glandular fever, or do I have Hodgkins disease?"

"You have Hodgkins disease," I told her.

"Thank you, Richard," she said. "God! They must have put you through hell!"

And she… she was better at facing what was happening to her than I was… Nothing is certain, I told her. We lead a charmed life… I clung to false hope! I had to! How could I not…?

In the last days, at the hospital… We were getting close on the bomb; we were working long hours, long days… And when I finally got to Arlene this one last time, she was very weak, and a bit fogged out… she didn't seem to know what was happening… She stared straight ahead most of the time, and she was trying hard to breathe. Every once in a while her breathing would stop, and then it would go on again… And I felt strange, sort of calm in a way. And as I watched her, I kept imagining all the things going on physiologically, the lungs not getting enough oxygen into her blood, making the brain fogged out, the heart weaker, which makes the breathing more difficult. I kept expecting some sort of avalanche, some dramatic collapse… but it didn't appear that way at all… she just got foggier… and her breathing became more shallow… until there was only one very small one… And when I kissed her for the last time, her hair smelled the same, which surprised me. Because, of course, in my mind, something enormous had just happened—and yet for a moment it seemed like nothing had happened.

And I left the room, and when I came back, the nurse was with her, and writing something down, the time of death... and I looked and saw the clock had stopped—at the exact moment of her death... And I thought, is that... is that possible? Is it some sign...?

Until I remembered, the clock had been stopping and starting a lot lately, and the nurse had obviously turned it to note the time of death; it was facing a different direction... In that moment, I wanted to believe in something. Some kind of magical thinking.

Arlene died four weeks before we finished the bomb. Four weeks before Trinity.

It was several months before I could react emotionally to her death. Not that I didn't feel it deeply. But it wasn't sinking in, until—isn't it interesting, how the mind works!—I was in Oak Ridge, and I was walking past a department store with dresses in the window, and I saw a pretty dress, and I thought, Arlene would like that. And then it hit me.

I don't know... suddenly it all came out... it was too much for me...

A couple years after she died, I wrote Arlene a letter. I told you about that. And I haven't looked at it for...

> *Pause.*
> *He crosses to the box.*
> *He takes the letter out of the box and stares at it.*

I haven't looked at it in over forty years.

> *He stares at the envelope.*
> *His eye wanders down to some papers on his desk.*

(He reads:) "Once upon a time a Wood Grouse and a Drake lived together. When it got cold the Drake would fly to warmer lands. The Wood Grouse would fly after him, weeping bitterly, and his eyes would swell and turn red. The Drake felt sorry for his friend. He plucked some blue feathers from out of his neck and some white down from under his wings and wrapped up the Wood Grouse to make him nice and warm. Since that time the Wood Grouse has had the same plumage as the Drake—blue on the neck and white under the wings...

The End."

Tuvan folk-tales don't appear to have that much meaning. At least, not on the surface. Not *under* the surface, either.

> *Pause.*
> *He opens the letter.*

My handwriting is so small!

(*Reads:*) "Arlene, I adore you, sweetheart… It is such a terribly long time since I last wrote you—almost two years but I know you'll excuse me because you understand how I am, stubborn and realistic, and I thought there was no sense in writing. But now I know my darling wife that it is right to do what I have delayed in doing. I want to tell you I love you. I always will love you.

You, dead, are so much better than anyone else alive.

> *He reads silently.*
> *Then:*

My darling wife, I do adore you.

I love my wife. My wife is dead.

P.S. Please excuse my not mailing this, but I don't know your new address."

> *He stares at the letter.*
> *He folds it carefully and puts it back in the box.*
> *Pause.*

I've been dreaming about her again lately. The other night, I dreamt she came to see me. "What are you doing here?" I said. "You're dead."

"I'm not," Arlene said. "I was only fooling. I got tired of you, so I went away for awhile. And now I've come back."

> *He lowers his head and sobs.*
> *He raises his head and wipes his tears.*
> *The phone rings.*
> *He lets it ring.*

MACHINE

Dick Feynman here.

Dr. Feynman, it's Dave Hackett again... You've probably gone home. Why don't we talk in the morning? We should make a decision tomorrow... Take the night, rest, and call me... I heard from some friends you were great in the show tonight... Talk to you...

Click.
Pause.

FEYNMAN
I'm not going to do the operation. It's time to simply let go.

He picks up the phone to call.

WOMAN'S VOICE (*Off*)
Professor...?

FEYNMAN
Oh God!

WOMAN'S VOICE (*Off*)
Can I come in?

FEYNMAN
No!

FIELD enters.

What are you doing here?

FIELD
I was walking home. I saw your light was on. All those photons of light streaming through your window. Oh, dear.

FEYNMAN
What's the matter?

FIELD
I broke my heel. I was dancing. In the grass. And I broke it. Anyway...

She takes off her shoes.

FEYNMAN

Miss Field?

FIELD

Yes?

FEYNMAN

Are you a little drunk?

FIELD giggles.

FIELD

Maybe. Just a little. I don't usually…

FEYNMAN

(*To audience:*) This might take a while. (*To FIELD:*) You're quite a dancer.

FIELD

Did we dance at the party?

FEYNMAN

Don't you remember?

FIELD

You drummed and I danced?

FEYNMAN

And then we talked about quantum mechanics.

FIELD

That I don't remember!

FEYNMAN

That's too bad. I explained it all to you!

She laughs.

FIELD

So where are they?

FEYNMAN

Where are what?

FIELD

Your etchings. You told me you wanted to show me your etchings.

FEYNMAN

I did? (*Laughs.*) That reminds me of a great Thurber cartoon. Guy's standing in the lobby of his apartment building, talking to a kind of homely-looking young lady. He says: "I got a great idea. Why don't you stay here… and I'll bring the etchings *down*!"

FIELD laughs.

FIELD

That's funny!

FEYNMAN

Yeah!

FIELD

Are you suggesting I'm homely-looking?

FEYNMAN

No, I'm not, Miss Field. (*Pause.*) I'm not. (*Pause.*) Not at all.

FIELD

What's the matter?

FEYNMAN

Nothing. It's just. In the moonlight. You look… like somebody I was just thinking about…

FIELD

Really?

FEYNMAN

Yeah. Somebody I knew a long time ago…

FIELD

This dress. I borrowed it. I'm not used to wearing it.

FEYNMAN

You look nice in that dress.

FIELD

Thanks. You look nice in your chief robe.

Pause.

So? Where are they?

FEYNMAN

Where are what?

FIELD

Your etchings.

FEYNMAN

(*Laughs.*) I was only joking!

FIELD

No, you weren't! I've seen your paintings. I've seen your drawings.

FEYNMAN

But I'm afraid right now isn't a very good—

FIELD

Is that your sketch pad?

FEYNMAN

Yeah, but don't look at it.

FIELD

These are beautiful!

FEYNMAN

They're not. They're just drawings.

FIELD

Yeah, and they're great! You owe me a picture, remember?

FEYNMAN

I do?

FIELD

Yeah. You said you wanted to paint me. As Nature.

FEYNMAN

(*Laughs.*) As Nature? I did? At the party?

FIELD

Weeks and weeks ago. Don't tell me you forgot?

FEYNMAN

No. I didn't forget.

FIELD

So draw me! And tell me about your lecture! "What You Know"!

FEYNMAN

What I know, huh? What I know and what I *think* I know…

FIELD

While you're painting my portrait…

She sits.

FEYNMAN

The thing is, what I know and what I *think* I know are sometimes very difficult to distinguish… When you realize that, you have a better chance of not fooling yourself…

FIELD

Fooling yourself?

FEYNMAN

It's like in quantum chromodynamics, for instance. The quarks. What you were asking me about earlier. See, we know that everything's made up of atoms, and we know that inside the atoms there's a nucleus with electrons going around it, and we understand the way electrons and photons interact…

FIELD

You understood it—*You* explained it—that what you won the Nobel Prize for! Solving QED!

FEYNMAN

Partly! Right! And *then* we began to understand how the nucleus itself works, and the subatomic particles *inside* the nucleus. And out of that we discovered fission, and made the bomb…

He stops.

FIELD

Dick…?

FEYNMAN

I'm sorry. I can't. I—I think you'd better go.

FIELD

Go? But why?

FEYNMAN

I'm sorry. I don't want to talk about it.

FIELD

(*Lightly:*) Is that what you do? Tell a girl you want to paint her, invite her up, and then send her away when you feel like it?

FEYNMAN

No, it's not! I *don't* do that! And I don't want to be doing this tonight at all!

Pause.

FIELD

I'm sorry. I'll go. It's silly, I guess. I was hoping to ask you earlier—when I came by—I was wondering if you thought somebody like me might have a future in science…

FEYNMAN

A future in science? That's a tough one. The question is, are you strong enough? Strong enough to always start from a place of doubt, and usually end up there? Strong enough to never be sure you're definitely right, but only be sure you're wrong?

FIELD

I don't know.

FEYNMAN

Well, that's good. Not knowing is at least a beginning.

FIELD nods.
She starts to go.

Miriam, I'm sorry. I didn't mean to be rough on you.

See, Nature has been dancing with me all my life. She's tantalized me, and sometimes I feel like I've gotten so close to her… close enough to lift her veil… but now I feel like I'm finished… I'm done for…

I haven't felt like this since… There was one other time. It was after the War. I was offered a job teaching at Cornell, and as I began to teach the course something wasn't right. Suddenly, when I tried to, I just couldn't get to work! It was driving me crazy! From the war, and my first wife's death… And everything else… I had worked so hard on the bomb… I had simply… burned myself out…

FIELD
And then?

FEYNMAN
What?

FIELD
I know this story.

FEYNMAN
Yeah?

FIELD
You told it once at a party I was at. There's more to it.

FEYNMAN
Well, everybody was expecting me to accomplish something. It was terrible.

FIELD
Yeah, but you got out of it somehow?

FEYNMAN
Well, finally I thought to myself, This is impossible to live up to—therefore, don't live up to it! You used to enjoy physics, I said to myself. Why not enjoy it again? Why not *play* with it?! *Amuse yourself! Have fun!*

She throws the frisbee.

Yeah… So within a week of feeling this way, I was in the school dining hall, when all of a sudden…

Some guy was fooling around. He throws a plate in the air. One of those plates with the university seal on one rim. As the plate goes up, I see it wobble, and I notice the red medallion going around, and it's pretty obvious that the plate's wobble is faster than its spin.

I figure out the motion. See, when the angle is very slight, the wobble is twice as fast as the spin—two to one. It turns out to be a pretty complicated equation! I tell Hans Bethe, and he says, "That's interesting, Feynman, but what's the *importance* of it?" And I say, "It has no importance! It's just for *fun!*"

But see, here's the thing. I went on working out various equations of wobbles. Then I thought about how electron orbits start to move in relativity, and about the path of least time in QED, and before I knew it, I was playing—working, really—in the same old way I used to… It was like uncorking a bottle.

And a lot of what I got the Nobel Prize for, years later, came out of piddling around with that wobbling plate!

> *He laughs.*

FIELD
Okay, that's more like it. You were so down in the dumps.

FEYNMAN
Well, it hasn't been the easiest day, Miriam.

FIELD
Then make it easier. Come on, let's dance! You got any music in this thing?

> *She turns on some music.*
> *She starts to dance.*
> *FEYNMAN watches her.*
> *Then, he puts a leaf in his hair.*
> *He starts to drum.*

FIELD
That's it! Act crazy!

FEYNMAN
Why not? I got a leaf in my hair.

> *He drums.*

He dances with her.
FEYNMAN drums, laughing.
She drums with him, laughing.
They dance, their dancing increasing into a frenzied frolic.
They collapse, laughing.
FEYNMAN stares at FIELD.
Pause.

FIELD

Now I think maybe I'd better go.

FEYNMAN

Yeah?

FIELD

Yeah. I think so.

FEYNMAN

I think so, too.

FIELD gathers her things.

FEYNMAN

You know, I was born not knowing things were made out of atoms, just like anybody else.

FIELD stops, looks at him.

I had to learn, just like anybody else. If you devote a great deal of time, and work, and thinking, and mathematics, you will become a scientist.

FIELD

Really?

FEYNMAN

Start with asking the simple questions. The ones that sound simple. What keeps the clouds up? Why can't I see stars in the daytime? Look at all the innumerable little things around you. And remember that everything is interesting if you look at it deeply enough. And then you'll do fine.

FIELD

Thank you. For a very *int-er-est-ing* evening!

FEYNMAN

You're welcome, Miss Field.

FIELD

Miriam.

FEYNMAN

I'll see you in class. And Miriam, thank *you*…

> *She smiles at him.*
> *She exits.*
> *Pause.*
> *He picks up the phone.*
> *He dials.*

Hackett?… It's Feynman… Did I wake you? Good… I've been thinking about it, and I think we should do it… Yeah… I think you should go back in… One last time… Let's flip the coin, and go for broke!… I'll talk to you tomorrow…

Oh, and one thing, Doc. I do have one request. If, during the operation, or even after, I start to go… please bring me out of the anesthetic…

Bring me out of it… Because I want to see what it's like… To die. It'll be an in-ter-est-ing experiment… If I'm going to die, I want to be there when I do!… Goodnight…

> *He hangs up.*
> *Pause.*

To summarize. "What We Know." This is the horrible condition of our physics today. Outside the nucleus, we seem to know a lot. This includes the domain of the very large, the planets and stars and galaxies, the universe as a whole. In this area, gravitation is the dominant force and Einstein's general relativity the triumphant theory. What we are pretty sure we understand also includes the second domain, everything in size between the planets and the nucleus, all of which come under the theory of quantum electrodynamics, QED, a theory of which we are justly proud. But the world of the very small—the tiny particles *inside* the nucleus… that world we lack a complete understanding of… Will we ever understand it?

We don't know. But not knowing is much more interesting than believing an answer which might be wrong.

We're lucky to live in an age in which we are still making discoveries… It's like discovering a new country… like trying to get to a strange, foreign place… a country almost beyond our imagining…

He picks up the phone. He dials.

Ralph? You there with Lebedev?… And Lamin? Yeah, it was great, man! A great performance!… Listen, I was thinking, Lamin mentioned something to us about our getting to Tuva through Novosibirsk… Well, I think you should try and get him to arrange that… Yeah, I think you should file for your visa… No, just yours, for now… Of course, sure, we're gonna go to Tuva together! Hold on one second.

He has a pain.
He puts down the phone.
He takes a pill.
He puts on the speaker phone.

Ralph?

RALPH'S VOICE
Yeah, Chief?

FEYNMAN
Remember what the Tuvan shaman says to the shepherd before he dies?

RALPH'S VOICE
I think so…

FEYNMAN
Would you say that for me?

Beat.

RALPH'S VOICE
"Don't cry. Don't be sad. All men must die, and you are not the first. Eat your meat, drink your arak; eat your millet, drink your tea…"

FEYNMAN
Thank you, Ralph. Thank you.

He turns off the speaker and picks up the phone.

So what are you going to do now? You still thinking about taking those guys to Las Vegas?... Sure, you should do it! They'd love it!... You tell them about the time I gambled with Nick the Greek?... *You* don't know *that* story?! Turn on your tape recorder! We could put it in the book!

He sits back in his chair and puts his feet up.
He turns on the Tuvan tape.

So, once, at the Flamingo, I met a few showgirls, struck up some conversation. So, pretty soon one of the girls says, "Let's go over to the El Rancho. Maybe things are livelier over there." So I get in their car with them, a very nice car, nice people, you know, and on the way over, one of them asks me my name.

The curtain starts to fall.

"Dick Feynman," I say. "Where are you from, Dick?" "Pasadena. I work at Caltech." "Caltech," one of them says. "Isn't that where that scientist Linus Pauling comes from?" Now... I've been to Las Vegas many times, and there was *nobody* who ever knew anything about science...

The curtain is down.